Living Worship—Living Praise

Obedience With a Thankful Heart

By GREGG SPILKER

TATE PUBLISHING, LLC

"Living Worship-Living Praise" by Gregg Spilker

Published in the United States of America
by Tate Publishing, LLC
127 East Trade Center Terrace
Mustang, OK 73064
(888) 361-9473

ISBN: 1-9331489-2-6

TABLE OF CONTENTS

FOREWORD

When Gregg first mentioned writing this book, I must admit I was hesitant to have too great of an expectation, not because he was incompetent of such, but rather because so often man sets out to do things with Godly intentions that lack the inspiration of the Lord. This nurtures man's idea and not necessarily God's divine plan. Fortunately, I knew the character of God within Gregg and I was most curious to see what would become of this project.

I must say; after he shared this book with me, I was so overwhelmingly delighted by the result that I refused to return the manuscript to him! Although it was just a rough copy, it has already become a favorite on my shelf, a constant reminder to seek after God's motives alone in all I do. This book beautifully divulges the true heart of worship in relation to welcoming the presence of God. It is the result of a life transformed by obedience as an act of worship and praise, just as God intended it to be. It is to be the entire focus of our daily walk with God and not merely a twenty minute portion of a Sunday morning service as it is sometimes limited.

Gregg has yielded himself to the Spirit of God, who has shaped his understanding through his willingness to embrace the only way to know true intimacy with our Master. Psalms 51:17 says, *"The sacrifices of God are a broken spirit: a broken and a contrite heart, O God, thou wilt not despise."*

I personally pray that God will give men and

women a hunger for this type of material that is often overlooked because many times as Christians, we seek after resources to propel *us* to greatness instead of those that revere God's greatness.

May you be richly enlightened as you discover the truths that follow, leading you to a deeper revelation of your purpose in Christ.

I am blessed to have the friendship of Gregg and his beautiful wife, Andrea. They have sacrificed much to see God's will fulfilled in their lives. May this be one of many successes that the Lord accomplishes through their lives, in the name of Jesus.

Looking to the cross,
Michelle Dunkley
Pastor, Kingdom Outreach

INTRODUCTION

I want to thank you for joining me in a wonderful walk in the Word of God. I believe that you want to have a closer walk with our creator. I believe that an area that so many people are lacking knowledge in is Worship and Praise. You may think you know and understand what they are, but in reality, you know only what you have been exposed to.

The purpose of this book is to broaden your understanding of Worship and Praise. Most people immediately think of church when addressing this subject. Though church does play a big part, it is not the only place worship and praise need to be discussed. Worship and praise should be the lifestyle of every single child of God.

I think one of the biggest rewards of this lifestyle is learning that when we live it, there are so many doors that we open to allow God to bless us in ways we never thought were possible. Our Father in Heaven wants to give us so many things, but we have to do our part in order to receive them. It is crucial to live in obedience with a thankful heart if we want to be blessed by our Father.

God has been speaking to me for a very long time on this subject. This book was born into my spirit about ten years ago. I did write a rough draft of this book then, but I had areas in my life that needed to be fixed before I could share them with you. There were things I didn't understand then that I understand now. I have had to grow-up in God and have had to learn more about Him in my own life.

What you hold in your hand is a very simple, yet very difficult key to understanding the Word of God and the nature of God. That statement almost sounds contradictory. Once your eyes are opened to the truth about worship and praise, you will see that it is a very simple truth. However, in order to reap the harvest of the seeds being sown, you will have to act upon the truth. This is where it becomes difficult. You will have to feed the seed. You will have to let it grow. There will be some immediate benefits from submitting to this truth, but the greatest harvest will come through time. Changing the way you act, think and feel.

I hope you enjoy this walk with me. It has been and continues to be a very interesting walk for me. As I listen to the voice of my Father and act according to His will, I know that miracles will happen. Life will be given to many who hunger and thirst after righteousness.

I also want to thank my wife for standing by my side through many hard times. She has shown me many times what it means to live a strong Christian life. Many times I see in her the love of the Holy Spirit and the compassion of our Lord. She is a beautiful person, inside and out.

Saving the best for last, I must thank my Heavenly Father, His son the Lord Jesus Christ and the precious Holy Spirit for giving me the knowledge and the ability to share this life-changing truth with you. God, and only God, could have ever known that I would be writing this to you and for you. To God be the honor and glory!

Come now and walk with me .

Chapter One:

In the Beginning

Worship and praise are more than songs and shouts of joy. They are more than feelings which engulf our emotions. They are more than mere words of proclamation or the thankfulness of salvation. Worship and praise is a lifestyle. It is a lifestyle of being obedient to our Father with a thankful heart in all things. Whether we are on the mountain top or in the deepest darkest valley, we can still be thankful.

In order to understand the true meaning of worship and praise, we will have to go back to the very beginning to learn who we are, why we are here, and where we are going. We will also see who God is and why He is the only one worthy of our worship and praise.

First let's take a walk in the garden.

Then God said, "Let Us make man in
Our image, according to Our likeness . . ."
Genesis 1:26

The Living Bible puts it like this:

Then God said, "Let Us make a man,
someone like ourselves . . ."

The following verse continues:

God made man like his maker,
like God did God make man;
Man and maid did he make them.

God created the heavens and the earth. God created everything there is, and after he created all these things, He then created his masterpiece, man, the most important part of creation, someone made in the fashion of Himself. Look at yourself in the mirror and see that the image looking back at you was formed inside and out in the exact likeness of Almighty God!

And the Lord God formed man
of the dust of the ground, and breathed
into his nostrils the breath of life; and
man became a living being.
Genesis 2:7

Just take a moment and let that sink into your soul. Just as God was, He made man to be the same way. God then looked at everything and saw that it was GOOD! Who are we? We are the creation to look like, act like, sound like and be like our creator.

God also created man for a purpose. He was created to have dominion over the fish in the sea, over the birds in the air, over the cattle, over all the wild animals and over everything else that creeps on the earth. God gave man the power to name everything and to be the master, the ruler of everything He had created. The Bible then tells us that God blessed man and told him to multiply and be fruitful. He also gave man every herb that yields seed and every tree whose fruit bears seed to eat.

As if that weren't enough, God took man and placed him in the Garden of Eden. God then told Adam and Eve that they could eat from every tree, except one. They could not eat from the tree in the midst of the garden, the tree of the knowledge of good and evil. You see, up to this point man had no knowledge of evil! Man had enjoyed all the beauty of creation, the oneness of man with God, the glory and the love. But as all of us know, this was soon to change.

But first realize that the choice from the very beginning was either to obey God or not. We all know that the choice Adam and Eve made was to disobey God and they chose to eat from the tree of knowledge of good and evil. And so it was in the beginning.

Read Genesis 3:22. How close to himself did God make man?

Then the Lord God said,
"Behold, the man has become like one of
Us, to know good and evil. And now, lest
he put out his hand and take also of the tree
of life, and eat, and live forever"—

Here we see that man became as God with the knowledge of good and evil. What would happen if he also ate from the tree of life and lived forever? This by no means, means that man would be equal to God, for only He is the author and creator. So what exactly happened when Adam and Eve sinned? Genesis 3:7 tells us that their eyes were opened and they knew they were naked. At this time their spiritual eyes were closed and their physical eyes were opened. They became separated from the glory they were living in and realized they were naked.

Then in the cool of the day, God came to walk with them in the garden. When they heard God coming to walk with them, they hid themselves from Him. Why? Because of fear! In other words, when Adam and Eve sinned, they came to know the feelings of shame and fear. How many people in this life are bound by the feeling of shame and fear? Two feelings which hinder so many from being what God intended them to be. They are two feelings which can hinder someone from feeling thankful, happy or fulfilled.

In Genesis 3:14–19 we see that when man sinned, God cursed the serpent, Eve, and Adam. From that point on, things have never been the same.

Take a look at the world around you. It is not a pretty sight. The curses which were put in place in Genesis are still in place today.

How far away from the way we were created have we come? What does this have to do with worship and praise? Is it possible to be what God intended us to be? I'm not talking about your ministry or your calling, but your life, my life! I am talking about our existence on this planet.

As God reveals himself to us, open your heart and your mind to revelation. Pray to see the truth. Search your life as I will mine to see what God would have for us. Together we will seek the meaning of true worship, true praise. A true knowledge of who we are, why we are and what we are going to become. Throughout this book, keep in mind that worship and praise is a lifestyle. You will understand why this is truth as we search the scriptures. As our spiritual eyes are opened, as we see where we are and where we need to be, are we going to be willing to become people of true worship and praise?

What did man do before he ate of the forbidden fruit? He walked with God and talked with God. God had a one on one relationship with man. It was personal. Before man disobeyed God, he saw God, in all of His glory and majesty. When man sinned, he broke that relationship with God. Man broke the bond between himself and God. To this very day man seeks to find a higher power, a god or a spirit greater than himself.

Why do we feel this need? Why is praise and

worship so important? Why are you important? And why does the human race fight so hard against the one who gives them life? How far away from the way we were created have we come? How far from the truth have we strayed? How far have we strayed from what God wants us to be and what he wants to give us? How weak has the church become and how strong can it become?

Walk with me through this journey. Find with me the truth of worship and praise. Become with me the man or woman God wants you to become, what He intended you to be.

I have been dumb-founded by the broad scope and the magnitude of what worship and praise are. It's hard to imagine all the areas that praise and worship affect and all the areas that affect worship and praise, even more importantly how praise and worship can change a life.

Throughout all of scripture, from Genesis to Revelation, God has made it clear that we are to obey His word and to give Him all the praise. How do we define praise and worship? Let's start with praise. Praise is about God. It can be addressed to others or to God. God himself, His attributes or His acts are the focus of our thoughts, our mind and our songs.

There is also corporate praise in the church. Gathering together because of the joy we have in Him. Praise exalts the Lord. We are dependent on Him.

Praise can be a celebration. It is a boasting of or acclaiming the greatness of God. The wonderful things He does and all the attributes that make him God. There can be singing, shouting and dancing before the Lord, being thankful for what He has done for us. It is being thankful for giving us victory in our lives. Praise is a confession of God. It is an attitude of thankfulness.

Praise, whether to God or about God, tells about His attributes or acts He performs. For example: "God is wonderful because . . ." or, "God, you are wonderful because. . . ." Though praise and worship are used in somewhat the same way, they are in fact very different.

Worship is made directly to God. Sometimes when we talk about worship we think about bowing down before Him, giving Him reverence or respect because of His deity, but just to bow down before him is not enough. Your heart must be in the right place because to worship also means to serve. How you feel in your heart and how you live your life will determine whether or not you worship the Lord. How do we live our lives in honor to Him? Simply put, by living in obedience to His word.

Is it easy? No! You must be committed to it. You see, there is a big difference between wanting something and committing to it. How do we commit to anything? It is by conviction, by believing in what you are doing. First we want something. Then we get convicted about it, and then we can commit to it. The conviction and the commitment come from your soul—the center of your being. Who or what is in the center of your life?

In the beginning, God was the center of Adam and Eve's lives. Every day God would walk with them and talk with them. They were taking care of everything that was created until they made the decision to disobey God. He was no longer the center of their lives. He was no longer their peace. They were no longer walking in His perfect glory.

Is God the center of your life? Do you want him to be? Do you want to be committed to exalting His name? The good news is that you can. You can have peace and joy and victory through our Lord Jesus Christ.

We can be changed. We can live the life God has for us. We can be holy and acceptable to Him. Praise the name of Jesus!

Why did God create the universe? Look at Revelation 4:11.

Thou art worthy, O Lord, to receive glory and honor and power: for thou hast created all things, and for thy pleasure they are and were created. (KJV)

All things were created for God's pleasure. The word pleasure here means to delight in, to desire, to love. All things were created for God to delight in. All things were created for God to love.

Why did God create man? Remember, God made man in His own likeness. After God created the heavens and the earth and everything in it, then He created man. God gave man dominion, to rule over everything He had created. God placed man the garden to share in the beauty, to delight in the creation, and to love the Creator. God desired to make man in His likeness so that man would desire God. God made man to love and to be loved in return. God wanted a relationship!

The reason things are today is the same reason they were in the beginning. You are here because God desires you to be here. You are here to be loved by God. You are here to delight the creator. You are here to desire the Father. You are here to love the Lord. You are here to delight in Him. You are here to give Him glory and honor. You are here to worship and praise the Almighty. You are here to serve and obey God with an attitude of thankfulness.

My dad once told me something that really touched my life and brought this home to me. He said that seeing his children serving God, being open to the Holy Spirit, listening to and obeying the will of our Father brings a joy to a father's heart that cannot be explained. I will never forget these words he spoke to me. If serving God can touch the heart of my earthly father in such a profound way, how much more my Heavenly Father must be pleased when I hear His voice and act according to His will? What better way to please your father than to live in obedience? What better way than to obey Him with an attitude of thankfulness because He chose you to do something for Him. What better motive do we need than to know that the creator of all things is pleased with you or me?

The choice we make, whether or not to obey God should be made at the time of salvation.

Therefore, if anyone is in
Christ, he is a new creation;
old things have passed away; behold,
all things have become new.
2 Corinthians 5:17

When you accept Jesus Christ as your personal savior, if you are truly going to follow Jesus, praise and worship are not options. When we become a "new creation," "old things have passed away . . ." The way we live has to change. "Behold all things have become new." These are changes in the way we see things, a difference in the way we think about things, difference in how we feel about things.

The "old things" which pass away is the natural way we think, feel and deal with life. They are our natural tendencies—what we say and how we act. When we "become new" we put on our spiritual life. Instead of living to please ourselves, we live to please our God. We see our sin, and we leave the sin behind. Instead of obeying the desires our own hearts, we obey the desires of our Father. When we become a "new creation," praise and worship become requirements, not choices. They are the demands of God on our lives.

Take a moment and look at Deuteronomy 5:7–15. Most of us know these as the Ten Commandments.

We are going to look at the first four commandments.

1. You shall have no other gods before Me
2. You shall not make for yourself any carved image . . . (Idols)
3. You shall not take the name of the Lord Your God in vain . . .
4. Observe the Sabbath day, to keep it holy . . .

Why did God spend more time on the first four commandments than on the following six? Why do the first four talk mainly about how to treat God? The reason is because God is our creator and must be placed as such in our lives. He should be the most important thing in our lives. He alone is worthy to be worshiped and praised!

Nothing in this life can be more important than God. Nothing in this life can be set as a higher priority than God. God's name is to be lifted higher than any other name. God is to be honored and revered. We are to remember Him and praise Him.

We are to place His will above our own. God must be first priority. Nothing should be placed as more important. Anything that becomes more important than God or anything that delays us from doing His will is considered as an idol. If God tells you to do something and you decide to do something else, you have set that thing above God! Do you realize that it could even be something that you feel is for God?

For instance, let's say there is a Christian concert you are planning to attend. At the same time, there is something else that God is telling you to do, like visiting someone who is sick or that you should spend time praying for a need God has placed on your heart. But, you decide to go to the concert. Which has become more important to you? The concert has taken priority over God, even though the concert was about God. When God tells us to do something, we must listen and be ready to do what He asks us to do in the time He wants it done.

> John 4:24 tells us;
> *God is Spirit, and those who worship Him must worship in spirit and truth.*

This is talking about two things. First is our spirit. When we refer to our spirit, we are talking about our innermost being. When we worship, it must come from our innermost self to God.

Secondly, we are to worship in truth. What is truth? Truth is simply this: to know the true nature of God. So in other words, when we worship God, we must worship from our innermost selves, knowing His true nature. Knowing who He is and how He wants things done, knowing that He is the ultimate authority over everything.

It's time for those of us who call ourselves "children of God" to start acting like it. We need to realize that we have a responsibility to God, ourselves, and the world to become true worshipers and to be a people of praise. So many people have fallen by the wayside because of a lack of joy and life in the church. Many have turned away because of petty disagreements over issues that are quite frankly, meaningless. Instead of focusing on our Lord Jesus Christ, the joy of the Holy Spirit, and looking to our Father in Heaven, we cut the throats of our brothers and sisters. We have turned countless people away, leaving them to fend for themselves, leaving them open for Satan to take their lives into an eternity without God.

But God is doing a wonderful work in the lives of so many in this world today. He is bringing us back to learning basic Bible teaching, Bible believing, and Bible doing. More people are searching for spiritual truth than ever before, and every day we are one day closer to the return of our Lord.

This is the day the Lord has made. So rejoice in it! Be glad in it! God is good all the time! Now let's enter His gate with thanksgiving and into the courts with praise! Enter into worship, the only one worthy of all our praise . . .

His Majesty:
The Lord Jesus Christ!

Chapter Two:

Praise - Living with a Thankful Heart

God is good, all the time! Nothing moves me more than to love the Lord and feel His anointing on and around me when I am in His presence. On the other hand, nothing makes me angrier than to be around someone who always sees the negative side of things. As one pastor put it, "No matter what situation you find yourself in, no matter how bad the circumstance, it's not Hell!" There is always a reason to praise the Lord. Even if the only reason to praise Him is because He is God! (Which I might add is all the reason we need.) Even in the valley, God is good!

Many Christians need to change their way of thinking in order to have a closer walk with God. Let's look at what it means to praise and who is praiseworthy. Some ways to define praise would be: to cheer, acclaim, endorse, admire, to pay tribute and to honor. Praising can be defined as: magnifying, glorifying, celebrating and exalting. Someone who is praise-worthy is admirable and excellent. To be excellent means to be first class, the finest, desirable, perfectly good and magnificent. So when we say we should praise the Lord, we can now say that we are honoring, glorifying, and exalting one who is excellent, the finest and perfectly good.

We ourselves have limited our belief in the power of God. We have put so many restrictions on God and then wonder why God doesn't move. "Bless me Lord, but don't ask me to change. Don't ask me to do something that makes me feel uncomfortable." We want God to live up to His promises, but we don't want to do what He wants us to do. Salvation is free to us. We don't deserve it. We can't buy it, but it stops there. In order to receive His blessings for our lives, we must obey His word. We must be willing to change. We must be willing to die to the flesh in order to live in the Spirit.

And whatever you do in word or deed, do all in the name of the Lord Jesus, giving thanks to God the Father through Him.
Colossians 3:17

You see, the Bible is filled with promises, but to reach the promise, sometimes you must go through battles. Sometimes you wait, but you must always follow the instruction God has given you. Through faith in overcoming the problem, you can walk in the provision God has for you, and in everything you do, give thanks!

Learning to praise the Lord in troubled times may be the hardest task to tackle. It is so easy to praise God in the good times. It's so easy to say how wonderful God is when you aren't in the midst of a trial. When an answer to prayer, no matter what it is, comes quickly, we are quick to give God the glory. But oh, when we are in the wilderness, when God seems so far away, where is the praise? When it seems impossible to make ends meet, where is the praise? What words come out of your mouth? Are you lashing out at a loved one, only making matters worse, or do you join together and pray believing in the answer and praising God for what He is going to do in your life? Do you focus on the problem or the answer?

I learned a valuable lesson in the summer of 1992. The Lord spoke to my wife and me and called us to Tennessee. I went one month before my family, in order to find a job and someplace to live. Due to a lack of finances, I set up in a campground. One month later my family joined me. For six months we lived in that campground in tents! We didn't have a trailer, no camper, no comforts of home. All the comforts of home were left behind. Believe me when I say that not everyone could understand how we could live in those conditions. I mean the dirt, the bugs, the RAIN! I think we had more rain that summer than I had ever seen! And even though I love to camp, six months was a true experience. But it was in this time that God changed my life so dramatically.

My whole family was changed that summer. We grew so much as a family. We learned to give God the glory, even when our tents and our whole campsite were torn apart by the rainstorm! Because of our living arrangements, so many people came to us feeling pity. They just couldn't understand how we could survive under these conditions. Understand also that during most of this time my wife and I did not have jobs and we were raising three small children. God had told us to go to Tennessee. So we left everything and moved, even without the prospects of work. But God would not let us down. We KNEW He wouldn't let us down! Talk about "faithing it." Most of the time we didn't even know where the lot rent was coming from! Yet, we stood fast; holding on to the promise God had given us.

As we stood faithful to Him, He was faithful to us. As God blessed us, we would bless God. As the money was provided, a portion was given to God first. Every single need we had was met. Not once did we go hungry. Not once did we go without a roof over our heads. Not once did God fail us! While some people were asking God "Why?" we were thanking God that we were all together as a family, attending a great church and anticipating what God had brought us here to do. Above all, we were learning how to give God all the glory and all the praise no matter what the circumstance.

Therefore by Him let us continually offer
the sacrifice of praise to God, that is,

the fruit of our lips, giving thanks to His name. Hebrews 13:15

I want to share another story with you. Sometimes it takes time to understand what God is teaching us. In November 1981 my wife and I were expecting the birth of our first child. We were living in Florida, and the only family we had living close to us were my grandparents. We were all so excited for this wonderful event to take place. The time came when my wife went into labor, so we all went to the hospital.

They took all of us into the waiting room. A short time later, a nurse came in to tell us what was going on. She said they were having trouble finding the baby's heart beat. We all began to pray that everything would be all right. At one point they even brought my wife in to be with us. I knew at that moment that something was wrong, but I kept hoping and praying that everything would work out right.

They finally took my wife into the delivery room. I can remember it like it was yesterday. The doctor came out to me and said, "I'm sorry, your baby is dead." My world came to a stand still.

I looked in the room where my wife was and I could hear her saying over and over to me, "I'm sorry! I'm sorry!"

All I could say to her was, "It's not your fault. I love you."

It was a beautiful baby boy. Perfectly formed, perfectly proportioned. The nurses themselves were saying how they had never seen such a perfectly formed child.

When I finally went home I began crying out to God. Why had this happened? What had I done to cause this? Was I being punished for things I had done? I didn't understand how God could have let this happen. We had been doing everything we thought God wanted us to do, so why?

Then, the first Sunday we went to church my grandmother said something to us, which at the time we didn't understand. She told us not to let the people see our pain. She said to be strong and let the people see you praise the Lord. Praise the Lord? After He allowed this terrible thing to happen to us? For a long time I thought that all she was concerned about was how it would look on the family. You see, my grand-parents were co-pastors in a church we had started. I thought she felt it would look bad on us if we went into church and people saw our sadness. Through the years I have learned that you can be sad, but you can still praise the Lord.

It wasn't easy, by any means, to sing happy songs. It wasn't easy to raise my hands. It wasn't easy to thank God. But I did and my wife did. God used this time to strengthen us. We became closer to each other and with God.

I did not understand this for many, many years. I did not know that God would use this as a way not only to teach me, but to teach you that you can give God praise, even in the dark valleys. He is our strength and our peace. No one else could say or do anything to help us, only God! We had to trust God—that He knew why, and His will would be done.

One year and nine days after this happened, our first daughter was born. We have been blessed with three beautiful daughters. And each time, God has let us know that He was with us every step of the way. Praise His Wonderful Name! This could have been a time that we just gave up. We could have lived the rest of our lives in depression, bound by the past, but by the grace of God, we have become conquerors! We are victorious!

Read the book of Job. I'm sure most of us are familiar with the story of Job. Job had a good life, but there was a time that he lost everything he owned as well as his entire family. And, like us, Job questioned God, and, just like us, God had to straighten Job out. But even though Job had lost it all, not having any reason to praise God, or even to live, he never once cursed God. He trusted God. In doing so, the man who had lost it all received a greater life than the one he had before. I don't know about you, but this says something to me. When you lose it all, when it looks like there is no reason to live, if you trust in the Lord and give it to Him, in return you can have a better life than the life you have had.

So many times we say things in anger or when we are frustrated. We lash out when things aren't going the way we want them to. Some of us are tired, weary from battling daily obstacles. Some of us are weak and hurt because of things others have said or done to us. All we want is some peace, some joy. Well, there is a way to be taken away. There is a way to peace, rest, and strength to go on. It is PRAISE!

Read again Hebrews 13:15. It tells us to "continually offer the sacrifice of praise . . . the fruit of our lips." Did you know that most of the time it is us who spoil the blessings that our Father has for us? Proverbs 18:21 says,

Death and life are in the power of the tongue,
And those who love it will eat its fruit.

Can we even begin to understand what God is saying here? Do we understand the importance of the things we speak? Look back one verse.

A man's stomach shall be satisfied from
the fruit of his mouth, and from the produce
of his lips he shall be filled.

Wow! Have you ever heard the saying "You are what you eat"? How about, "You are what you speak"?

Either you are eating life or you are eating death. You are feeding yourself everything that is coming out of your mouth. And where do the words you speak come from? Matthew 12:34 tells us, it's from your heart.

. . . For out of the abundance of the heart, the
mouth speaks.

If your heart is filled with hatred, bitterness, anger, unforgiveness, etc., then that is what you will speak. If you fill your heart with lust, envy, immorality, etc., then that is what you will speak. What about sickness, depression or fear?

Whatever you put in your heart will find its way out of your mouth. And as you speak, you are filling yourself with it. Sure, you might be able to fool people for a little while, but it will show up. It WILL come out! Probably when you least expect it. And when you speak it, you are putting it right back into your spirit, where it is coming from in the first place. It then becomes a vicious never ending cycle. If you want to be victorious in your life, the cycle must be broken. Maybe the reason you aren't victorious is because of what you are feeding yourself!

Let me say now that the cycle can be broken. You can stop speaking death in your life. You can be free from the diet that is killing you. You can learn how to speak life into your soul.

Keep your heart with all diligence, For
out of it spring the issues of life.
Put away from you a deceitful mouth
And put perverse lips far from you.
Let your eyes look straight ahead,
And your eyelids look right before you.
Ponder the path of your feet,
And let all your ways be established.
Do not turn to the right or to the left;
remove your foot from evil.
Proverbs 4:23–27

Praise God! What a recipe for a successful life! You know, it is just like our physical well-being. I know someone who was recently diagnosed with diabetes and high blood pressure. The doctor gave him specific instructions on what to eat and what not to eat. What to do, what not to do. This is exactly what God is doing here. Let's take a moment and take a closer look at this passage.

Keep your heart . . . Pay attention to your heart. Watch what you are thinking, at all times. Why? The reason is this, because out of your heart *spring the issues of life.* How you feel in your heart rules your life. If you keep your heart in the right place, if you seek God continually, and if you hide His word in your heart, then you will live. If your heart is always full of God, you will speak life. You will feed yourself life.

Put away from you a deceitful mouth . . . Stop being deceived by your own words. Stop lying to yourself and everyone around you. *Put perverse lips far from you . . .* Stop listening to and speaking twisted truths. Stop looking for someone to tell you what you want to hear. John 14:6 says,

"I am the way, the truth and the life . . ."

Stop listening to the lies of the world and start listening to Jesus!

Look straight ahead . . . Do not be enticed by the things around you. Don't be enticed by the people around you. 2 Timothy 2:22 tells us,

Flee also youthful lusts; but pursue righteousness, faith, love, peace with those who call on the Lord out of a pure heart.

So many times in our daily lives we get caught up by the things around us. We begin to look at the situation instead of looking toward God. So many times when we are confronted by a situation, or even just daily problems, we throw our hands in the air and surrender to defeat, and then ask ourselves where God is. If we had been looking straight ahead toward God, giving Him the praise, and knowing that He is our strength, we may have noticed that the problem really wasn't a problem at all! It is just one more thing that our God is bigger than!

Thy word is a lamp unto my feet, and a light unto my path. Psalm 119:105 (KJV)

For the commandment is a lamp
And the law is light . . . Proverbs 6:23(KJV)

Ponder the path of your feet and let all your ways be established. We must know the word of God. We must follow His instructions. We must be established. God will never leave you alone in the darkness. Sometimes it feels that way—like God has forgotten us—but He is right there. Sometimes it is because we have wandered off the right path. Perhaps because of our circumstances, our focus has become blurred. We must be established! If God tells you to do something, do it! If God tells you to wait, then wait! Get to know His voice. Stop listening to the voices along the way that are trying to get you off the road to Glory! BE ESTABLISHED!

Do not turn to the right or the left . . . The road is straight and narrow, but there are so many roads along the way. There are wide roads, hilly roads, and curvy roads. I want you to know this: all roads lead to a dead end, every road except one, the Cross road. Follow the commandments and laws of the Lord, stay focused on Him, and stay on the straight and narrow road that leads to eternal life, forever with our Lord.

Remove your foot from evil. Don't play around with the world. You cannot have one foot in the world and one foot toward Heaven. You cannot serve two masters. God will not tolerate this kind of lifestyle. If something comes along that tempts you, get away from it! If someone is trying to get you to stray from God's plan for your life, get away from them! Keep yourself focused on God and God alone!

Why is it important to praise? Remember that with the tongue we speak life or death. We speak blessing or curse.

A merry heart makes a cheerful countenance,
But by sorrow of the heart the spirit is broken."
Proverbs 15:13 (KJV)

A wholesome tongue is a tree of life,
But perverseness in it breaks the spirit.
Proverbs 15:4 (KJV)

A merry heart does good like medicine,
But a broken spirit dries the bone.
Proverbs 17:22

Remember what we said earlier; when we give God the praise, He gives us joy. The joy of the Lord is our strength. Without praise, without joy, we are going to dry up, wither, and die! We must make a conscious decision every day to praise the Lord. We must learn to guard our tongues!

Whoever guards his mouth and tongue
Keeps his soul from troubles.
Proverbs 21:23

The third chapter of the book of James is so clear about controlling the tongue. In fact, it says that if you can learn to control the tongue, you can control the rest of your body to do what it should. We will take a closer look at this when we talk about worship.

So, we find that if we know the word of God and it is in our hearts, then out of the abundance of our heart we will speak life into our lives. When we are full of God, when we praise Him, He gives us joy. The best part of this is when our cups run over with the joy of the Lord; it will spill out onto everyone we come in contact with. People will see God in our lives. He will be exalted! He will be glorified! This is what praise is all about!

God desires a one-on-one relationship. Why else would He have created a man in His very own likeness? Why else would He walk and talk to man in the garden? We must realize that God expects us to live a holy life. We need to realize that the Lord Jesus Christ is the great "I Am," and that we should bow down before His throne and Worship Him!

Holiness is a dirty word to many, but God said that when Jesus returns for His bride, it is to be without spot or wrinkle. It is not just a Sunday morning ritual. The only way for the church to be ready for His return is for us to live a holy life everyday of our own daily lives, twenty-four hours a day, seven days a week.

In Philippians 3:12 (NCV) the Bible reads like this,

I do not mean that I am already as God would have me to be. I have not yet reached that goal, but I continue trying to reach it and to make it mine. Christ wants me to do that, which is the reason He made me his.

Am I a failure if I stumble? No! I have not reached the goal of being everything God wants me to be, but I do have a goal to be everything He wants me to be. And I will continue to reach for that goal until it is mine! Have I conquered the things I say, controlling my tongue at all times? No! But my goal is to control it at all times. Am I thankful at all times? No! But it is my goal to be thankful at all times. It is my goal to live my life on earth the way Jesus did and to become more and more like Him everyday. It is my goal to give Him all the praise, all the time!

Many battles in the Bible were not fought with weapons but by praise. In Deuteronomy chapter 33, Moses blesses the tribe of Judah. One definition of Judah is praise. Verse 7 says,

". . .Hear, Lord, the voice of Judah, And bring him to his people; let his hands be sufficient for him, And may You be a help against his enemies."

One example of a battle being won by praise is found in 2 Chronicles 20:20–24. Judah was going to war and Jehoshaphat gave the people a word from the Lord. Beginning in verse 20,

" . . . Believe in the Lord your God, and you shall be established; believe his prophets, and you shall prosper."

Then Jehoshaphat appointed those who would go BEFORE the army and SING to the Lord, and PRAISE the beauty of His holiness saying,

"Praise the Lord for His mercy endures forever."

Do you know what happened? When the people of Judah began to sing and to praise, the Lord set ambushes against those who were coming against

Judah. The enemies killed each other and themselves. NO ONE had escaped!

Isn't this exciting? When the enemy comes against you, if you can learn to sing praise, you may not even have to fight the battle! God will make the enemy destroy itself!

Every day we are attacked by the powers of Hell trying to steal our souls from eternal life with our Heavenly Father. The closer we get to our Lord's return, the more intense the attacks become. The closer we walk with Jesus, the more the powers of darkness try to cause us to fall.

So many people only see Jesus as the tiny babe lying in a manger. Some only see Him as a great teacher or prophet. Some only see Him as a man hanging on a cross. But, praise God! He was the Son of God who did come and teach, and He gave His life on the cross to save us from our sins. Yet, the story doesn't end there. HE AROSE FROM THE DEAD! He went into the pits of Hell and met Satan face to face! Jesus took the keys of death, Hell, and the grave right out of the Devils hands! Jesus Christ lives today! He reigns as King of Kings and Lord of Lords, forever! He is coming back as the bridegroom, coming to take His beautiful bride away!

Revelation 19:11 does not describe Jesus lying in a manger, nor the one silently being tortured and crucified, but rather as the conqueror with eyes like the flames of fire, wearing many crowns. He is wearing a robe dipped in blood, and out of His mouth comes a sharp sword, with the name King of Kings and Lord of Lords on his robe and on his thigh.

But until He does return, it is our job, our responsibility to take back the land Satan has stolen away. We must break down the walls that keep us from Him. We must learn to be victorious.

Do you want to be an overcoming warrior? Do you want to quit living in defeat? If so, you must submit yourself to change. If the Devil can keep you down, if depression can take hold in your life, if you speak how bad things in your life are, you will live in defeat. But, when you feel like giving up, when you ask yourself if it is all worth it, ask yourself this one question. Is it worth losing your soul, being without God for all of eternity?

This is when you must hold to the promise of God. You will be protected under the shadow of the Almighty. You are His child. No one loves you like your Heavenly Father. If every day you are in a battle you fight the same way, you will stay in the same place. Perhaps a new plan of attack is necessary.

Instead of confessing how bad things are, thank God for what He has already done, what He is doing, and what He is going to do in your life. Set your goal. Be established. Speak positive and speak praise. You are not on the verge of disaster; you are on the brink of a miracle! Hallelujah! To God be the glory! When you begin to praise His holy name, trials seem to become much smaller. When you begin to love Him, He will love you right back.

When you say, “Lord, I can’t make it on my own,”

He will say in return, “You don’t have to fight alone. For I, the Lord God, am on your side. I will never leave you, nor forsake you.”

When things get you down, lift your hands, lift your voice, and most of all;

JUST KEEP PRAISING HIM!!!

Chapter Three:

Worship - In Spirit and in Truth

I believe that more than anything, God wants to have a one on one relationship with us. He wants to be able to touch us and bless us in ways we never dreamed possible. I believe He wants us to be able to enter a holy place. But before we can enter this holy place, we must first pass through the courts of praise, even in our prayer life when we bring our needs before the Lord.

Be anxious for nothing, but in everything by prayer and supplication, with thanksgiving, let your requests be made known to God;
Philippians 4:6

So many times we come to God only to ask Him for something—to answer a want or need in our lives. We want Him to help us unconditionally. Yet every day we try solving our problems the way we think they should be solved. Let's be honest; we all do this. And then, when things fall apart, we go crying to God, asking Him why things have gone wrong. Perhaps we need to listen to what God wants us to do, how He wants the situation handled.

"I also gave them this command:
Obey me, and I will be your God and you
will be my people. Do all that I
command so that good things
will happen to you."
Jeremiah 7:23 (NCV)

God wants us to rely on Him. He wants us to ask what He wants. He wants to be thanked for what He does. He wants us to listen to Him when He speaks. He wants to be part of our lives, the most important part of our lives. He wants to be the center of our lives, and he wants to be worshiped.

What is worship? Most of us understand the Hebrew form "shachah" which means to depress, i.e. prostate as in homage to royalty or to God, to bow down. In Greek the word for worship is "proskuneo" which means to adore or give reverence to. If we will dig deeper, we will also find that another word for worship is the Greek word "latreuo" which means to do the service of . . . to serve. We cannot limit worship as just a practice of bowing down before God but as a lifestyle of doing His service, a lifestyle of obedience.

Let's take a moment and look back at the temple that we're told about in the Old Testament.

Outside of the temple were courts. This is where most of the people would gather for prayer, presenting their sacrifice to the Lord, and as they made their sacrifice, they would sing songs of praise. Inside the temple is an area known as the Holy Place. This area was reserved for priests and worship leaders. Then beyond the Holy Place is a room known as the Holy of Holies. This was the place that only the high priest was allowed to enter. This is the place that the high priest would pray to God for the forgiveness of all the people.

The high priest could not have any sin in his life when he entered into the Holy of Holies. Before the priest entered this sacred room he would have a rope tied around his waist. At the bottom of his robe were bells. As long as the people could hear the bells on the priest, they knew that he was praying to God to forgive them. But if the bells became silent, this meant that the priest had sin in his life and he died! Then they would have to drag him out with the rope, and another priest would have to enter to pray.

What do you consider to be sin? I believe the best definition of sin is this: anything that is disobedience to God. I believe that this will answer many questions you may have in your life. Do you realize that you could actually be doing a good thing, but if God told you not to do it, it is sin? And you cannot have an intimate relationship with God if you have sin in your life. So how do we get to the place of having a relationship with God? By worshiping Him! Jesus said in John 4:24,

"God is Spirit, and those who worship Him must worship in spirit and truth."
The verse prior to this says,
"But the hour is coming, and now is, when the true worshipers will worship the Father in spirit and truth; for the Father is seeking such to worship Him."

Now is the time that the Father is seeking who? He is seeking true worshipers! And how do they worship? In spirit and truth! Do you remember what we said earlier about worshiping in spirit and truth? It means to worship from our inner-most being to God's spirit, knowing the true nature of God. In other words, God is looking for a people who will know Him and His ways and who will live in obedience to Him with all of their being!

In order to truly worship the Lord, you must know who He is! It must become real to you. When His holiness and awesomeness becomes real to you, then you will be ready for His life changing power to come and cleanse and purify your life! When you submit yourself to His will, you will begin to walk in worship to Him. You will walk in obedience.

When you give yourself to God, you must give Him all of you: your thoughts, your feelings, your physical body, and your own will! In other words, how you live your life will show whether or not you truly worship the Lord. You must believe He is who He says He is in order to give yourself to Him. Why else would you commit your life to Him?

Why do you think so many in this day and age are giving themselves over to the New Age Movement? They are being drawn in part by being told they can do anything in themselves. They are in fact, God! Yes, you must believe in yourself, but this is going much further! You must have a healthy self-esteem, but you are not God! This is a lie from the pit of Hell! This is the same lie that the serpent told Eve in the Garden of Eden when he told her that if she ate of the forbidden fruit, she would be the same as God! It's hard to believe that this same lie is still deceiving millions of people today. You do not have the power to make it on your own. You cannot withstand the powers of evil without the power of the Almighty!

In order to worship in spirit and truth, we must live in obedience. This means obedience in all aspects of our lives. When God tells us to do something, we must do it. If not, we are not committed to Him completely and thus we are not worshiping Him. When we disobey God, it is sin. God cannot dwell in sin, for God is holy and where He dwells must be holy.

I can hear some of you now. You are thinking, "There's no hope for us. We are not perfect and we cannot become perfect."

To you I say, "WRONG"! Yes, it is true that we are born into this world where sinning is natural to the flesh. However, we can become perfect through the blood of Jesus! Thank God for His mercy that passes all understanding. The blood of Jesus covers it all!

This is why the Father sent His Son, to give us life, to take sin out of our lives. This is the power of the blood of Jesus! It cleanses us from all unrighteousness. When we accept Jesus as Lord and Savior of our lives, the Father sees us through the blood of His only begotten son.

. . . For He has covered me with the robe of righteousness . . . Isaiah 61:10

To become righteous means to live according to the standards set forth before us in the Word of God. When Jesus died, He took upon himself the sin of the world: past, present and future. When Jesus was on the cross, do you know why the Father turned away from looking at His Son? The Father could not look at Jesus because Jesus took on all of our sin. He could not bear to see His Son covered in all the sins of the world. Even though Jesus himself never sinned, God treated Him that way. Jesus did this all so you and I could have eternal life!

In the same way, when we accept Christ into our lives, the Father looks at us as clean, pure, and righteous. When we come to God for redemption, He sees us as perfect, for our sins are covered by the Lamb of God. When we come to the cross for salvation, our sins are washed away by the blood of Jesus. God does not remember our sins of the past.

He doesn't hold them against us at a later date. When we are redeemed, we are redeemed!

So, can we become perfect? The answer is a great big, YES! We can become without sin in our lives. Why else in John chapter 8 would Jesus tell the woman at the well to go and sin no more? Jesus was not playing a mind game with this woman! He was saying to her to go and not to practice the lifestyle of sin, which she had been living.

Please take time to read 1 John 3:4–10. This puts the whole thing in black and white.

. . . Whoever sins has neither seen
Him nor known Him.
1 John 3:6

Whoever has been born of God does not sin,
for His seed remains in Him; and he cannot
sin, because he has been born of God.
1 John 3:9

Once again I feel it is important to talk about our speech as well as our actions. Please take time to read the entire third chapter in the book of James. But before you do this, look at what James 1:25–27 says to us.

But he who looks into the perfect law
of liberty and continues in it, and is not a for-
getful hearer but a doer of the work, this
one will be blessed in what he does.

If any among you thinks he is religious, and does not bridle his tongue but deceives his own heart, this one's religion is useless.
Pure and undefiled religion before God and the Father is this: to visit orphans and widows in their trouble, and to keep oneself unspotted from the world.

Well my friends, there it is in a nutshell. We must look and continue in the perfect law of liberty, and do what we should do, and then God will bless us. We must bridle our tongues or else everything else we do is useless. It also tells us to be unspotted before the world.

Now look at James, chapter three. We must learn to bridle our tongues. Remember that we either speak blessings or curses, life or death. Verse 6 tells us that the tongue "is a fire, a world of iniquity," and "it defiles the whole body."

Verses 9–12 once again talk about a split lifestyle or "forked-tongue" if you will. With our tongue we give God praise and bless God, yet at the same time, we are cursing man. Both blessing and cursing from the same tongue, and the Bible says, "This should not be so." Like a spring of water, it cannot give both fresh water and salty water. You must choose which path you will follow. But remember, you cannot and will not survive with one foot toward heaven and one in this world (or should I say one foot toward Hell).

We must learn how to come out from among

them and separate ourselves from them. We must begin a new life of "joy unspeakable and full of glory"!

For "He who would love life
And see good days,
Let him refrain his tongue from evil,
And his lips from speaking guile (lies);
Let him turn away from evil and do good;
Let him seek peace and pursue it.
For the eyes of the Lord are on the righteous,
And His ears are open to their prayers;
But the face of the Lord is against
those who do evil."
1 Peter 3:10–12

What is this saying to us? I believe our focus has become blurred, or perhaps some have even turned away from the teaching of holiness and righteousness. So many people these days are so wrapped up in themselves that they cannot, and will not see the error of their ways. People don't want their toes to get stepped on. As long as the preacher speaks on things that make them feel good, everything is fine. But if they get out of their "safe-zone," when the Holy Ghost reveals sin in their lives, watch out! People leave the church or vote the pastor out, denying the truth. They would rather find somewhere else or someone else that would make them feel good.

When will people understand, WE MUST BECOME HOLY! God cannot live where there is sin. Salvation is free to all who will believe in Jesus, but to grow and to become spotless before God will cost everything. It is not an over-night thing. It is a daily walk with God, becoming mature in the things of God and obeying Him. It means that you may lose some of your friends. It may mean that you lose your present job. It may even mean that you lose close family ties, just because you choose to follow God.

I remember when we decided to follow God and move to Tennessee. We were so excited! Our anticipation of where God was leading us and what He would do with us was overwhelming, and we were sharing our joy with our families. The fact that we were moving wasn't a problem. The fact that we were going to be involved with a church outside of our denomination was horrible to them. We were practically accused of joining a cult! They did not want to hear if they believed the same or not. Well, praise God for His love and mercy!

We did not abandon anything! We just decided to follow God's will for our lives! Growing up, I was given a foundation from God's word. I was taught to follow God no matter where He would lead me, and I was taught to strive to be more like Jesus. Well, Jesus did not belong to one group of people, did He? Jesus came for all mankind. God has led me and my family to this glorious place to grow. I prayed to be more like Jesus. I prayed that I would learn to truly worship Him. I prayed that God would change my life, and He has! In fact, He is still teaching me, showing me, and changing me! Hallelujah!

Believe me when I say, it is not an easy road

to travel. But the reward for traveling the straight and narrow is greater than the imagination can conceive! The greatest reward is to know that we will be with God, in His presence forever! The best part of this reward is that we don't have to wait to be in His presence. We can dwell in His presence every day, right now, no matter where we are!

But to receive this reward, we must also learn to listen. We must learn to hear the voice of God. We must learn to obey the voice of God.

Many times in a church service, God will give us a taste of what He desires to give us. The Holy Spirit begins to move in lives, and people let go of their problems, whether it be sickness or anything else that stands between them and God, that is when God can bless His children. This is why many are healed during a worship service, because their eyes are on the Healer and not the disease!

I also believe that this is why so many have a hot/cold relationship with God. One Sunday they are in church praising and worshiping God. They have their heart right with Him, all the cares of this world are behind them, and they are completely focused on God. Then something happens later that day or even before they get out of the church, and automatically they focus on the problem instead of the Mighty God they just got finished worshiping! We must learn to give God everything, all the time! Remember, whatever is in the heart . . .

Therefore "come out from among them and be separate, says the Lord. Do not touch what is unclean, and I will receive you." "I will be a Father to you, and you shall be my sons and daughters, says the Lord Almighty." 2 Corinthians 6:17, 18

Therefore, having these promises, beloved, let us cleanse ourselves from all filthiness of the flesh and spirit, perfecting holiness in the fear of God.
2 Corinthians 7:1

And everyone who has hope in Him purifies himself, just as He is pure.
John 3:3

Can this be any clearer? We must become the holy church, without spot or wrinkle. God will not accept a blemished bride. Even in the Old Testament when sacrifices were made, the animal being sacrificed had to be perfect, without blemish! This is why God sent Jesus. A perfect sacrifice without blemish! God's very best! Jesus was pure, clean, and holy. And though He was blameless, He gave his life just so we could be free and we would be able to have a one on one relationship with God again!

Worship in spirit and truth! Live in obedience! Separate yourselves! Become holy! Do not touch the filthiness of the flesh! Two things God told man to do: worship and praise! Live in obedience and do it with a thankful heart!

If you can get this into your spirit, you will

never, never be the same! What does God want from you? Praise - all the time! Worship - all the time! ALL THE TIME!

Some who read these words will become defensive, self-righteous or possibly even angry. Get rid of the religious spirit that is keeping you from living a victorious life! Learn the truth! Get out of your bondage and get into victory! These are not my words, but the words of the Lord! Search the scriptures. Try them, test them. Depart from anything that is between you and God. In mercy and truth atonement is provided. How can anyone explain how great God's love is for each one of us?

In mercy and truth atonement is provided for iniquity; and by the fear of the Lord one departs from evil.
Proverbs 16:6

God will not fail you. Get rid of the weight of sin! Let God take the shackles off your feet and dance before the Lord. Take off the hand cuffs and raise your hands in surrender to God. Let God take the weight of the world off your shoulders and jump for joy! Take the darkness off your heart and mind and fill them with the light of the Word and worship the Lord in spirit and truth! Hallelujah! Give God the glory due His name!

You have a choice. The key is in your hand. The key is in the lock, but the door will not open until the key is turned to unlock the door. Will you turn the key? Will you unlock the door? Will you give the Holy Spirit access to your life? Will you open your life to the joy-filled victorious life God has for you? It's up to you! You have the knowledge, now what are you going to do with it?

God will not do anything unless you allow Him to come in and do His work. God has called to His people. Who will listen? Who will choose to walk on the good road? Choose this day who you will serve.

This is what the Lord says: "Stand where the roads cross and look. Ask where the old way is, where the good way is, and walk on it. If you do, you will find rest for yourselves. But they have said, 'We will not walk on the good way.'"
Jeremiah 6:16 (NCV)

Chapter Four:

Worship and Praise the Lord God Almighty!

Throughout this book we have used words like God, Almighty, Lord and many others. It is important to know who we are talking about. You may even use these words in your daily life, yet you still find yourself living in defeat. You still struggle from day to day. Maybe the reality of who God really is has not become real to you.

I have no doubt that you believe there is a God and He sent his son Jesus to free you from your sins. But what about sickness, financial problems, broken families, depression, alcoholism or anything else that would bring distress in your life? The list seems endless. God's mercy endures forever! I hope that the Holy Spirit helps me in this chapter to bring forth the reality of God's identity, the reality that we serve a God who created this world. He is the God who saves, heals, delivers and will never, never let you down.

This question was posed earlier: Why would anyone commit their life to something or someone who wasn't real to them? When you trust in someone, you believe that whatever it is that you trust them to do, they will do. You have no doubt in your mind that they can complete the job from beginning to end. You believe that whatever they say is true. The promises they made to you are going to be kept.

When you ask Jesus into your life, He is real to you. He is real to you as the Savior, the Lamb of God who gave His life to free you from your sins. It is real to you that through the power of the blood of Jesus, you can have everlasting life. It is real that no matter what you have done in your life, it is forgiven and that God is going to free you from the bondage of sin you have been living under. You believe that He loves you!

Many people still see Jesus as the babe in the manger. Some people have never gone past this awesome gift from the Father. Too many people focus on the Virgin Mary, instead of the One to whom she gave birth, the gift she allowed herself to bare. Mary did find favor with God, but Mary cannot save you. She cannot bridge the gap between man and God. She cannot heal. She cannot deliver. She was just a willing vessel that allowed God to use her. The focus of the birth must be Jesus!

Jesus was born in a stable and was laid in a manger, but this is only the beginning of the last sin sacrifice. This was not the birth of a great teacher. It was not the birth of a great prophet. This was the birth of the Savior! The birth of God made man! This was the beginning of a one-on-one relationship with man once again!

There are so many names for the Lord Jesus Christ. I cannot begin to cover them all. I want to give you enough to stir your spirit so you will begin to search out who He is in your life. He is not a historic figure, but a living being that is right by your side - all the time.

In the beginning was the Word and the Word
Was with God, and the Word was God.
John 1:1

This is a very familiar verse for many Christians. The term "Word" refers to Jesus. In other words, before the physical birth of Jesus, He was and always has been. In the beginning was Jesus.

The second part of the verse says, " . . . and the Word was with God . . ." This refers to the Trinity. They are three separate individuals, yet they are one God. One does not operate without the other. The Trinity consists of the Father, the Son (Jesus) and the Holy Ghost. So in this part of the scripture it tells us that Jesus was with the Father and the Holy Ghost.

The last section of this verse says, " . . . and the Word was God." This tells us that Jesus is in fact God, which in itself verifies the second part of the verse.

Now when you put it all together, it reads like this: "In the beginning was Jesus, and Jesus was with the Father and the Holy Ghost, and is in fact, God." The birth of Jesus was not the beginning of His existence. He has always been and He will always be!

Before we go any further let's understand that the Bible is not just a book of fables; it is in fact, the Word of God. It was given by God and written by men used as willing vessels of God. The Bible is truth! In it you will learn the true nature of God. In it you learn what God wants, what He desires, what He has done, and what He is going to do.

In the first book, in the very first verse, the Bible talks about the Father, the Son and the Holy Ghost. It says, "*In the beginning God* **. . .**" How do I know it is talking about the Trinity? Look back at Genesis 1:26. God said, "*Let US make man in OUR image . . .*" This clearly shows that there was more than one person, yet only one God. The story of Jesus does not begin in Matthew 1:1, but actually before Genesis 1:1. He has always existed! HE IS GOD!

In Isaiah 7:14 it was prophesied that a virgin would give birth to a son and she would call him Immanuel. Matthew 1:21–23 shows this as being fulfilled. Immanuel translated means "God is with us." So God, who always was, came to us in body as a physical being to be with us.

Throughout His whole life, Jesus never committed a sin. He was tempted, yet He never gave in to sin. As a human being, He has felt every single thing that we have felt. Yet, He still lived a perfect life!

How did He do this? And if He can do it, why can't we? Why do so many Christians still live in defeat?

Let's look a little closer at the Trinity. There is a very well known pastor who explained the Trinity so well. I am going to try to explain what he said that has helped me so much in understanding how the Trinity works. One example goes something like this: God the Father speaks the word, "Let there be light." God the Son (Jesus) flips the switch. God the Holy Ghost is the power, the electricity, which causes the light to come on. There is one who speaks the word, one who performs the action, and one who is the power.

You must have all three elements in order for the light to come on. If the Father said, "Let there be light," and no one flipped the switch, there would not be light. In the same token, if the Father said "Let there be light" and the Son flipped the switch but there was no power, no electricity, there would still not be light. You must have all three in order for the light to come on. So, in the creation of the world, the Father spoke the word, the Son performed the act with the power of the Holy Ghost. "GOD" created the heavens and the earth.

Jesus, in His life on earth, was never without the Father and the Holy Ghost (Spirit). John 5:19 says that Jesus could not do anything of himself, but what He sees the Father do, for as the Father does, the Son does in like manner. When Jesus was baptized by John, the Bible says that the Spirit of God descended upon Jesus like a dove and remained on

Him. God had told John that when he saw this, this would be the one who would baptize with the Holy Spirit.

When you look at the crucifixion of Christ, you will see all of God in action. The Father sent his only begotten Son to die for our sins. The Son came to earth and laid down His life and died on the cross to free us from the bondage of sin. And, by the power of the Holy Ghost, Jesus rose up from the dead! Even in the life and death of Jesus, all of God was present. Now look and see what the Bible tells us in Romans.

But if the Spirit of Him who raised Jesus from the dead dwells in you, He who raised Christ from the dead will also give life to your mortal bodies through His Spirit who dwells in you. Romans 8:11

Wow! This is telling us that the same Spirit (the Holy Spirit) who raised Jesus from the dead dwells in us! As Christians, we have the same Spirit in us! And because He lives in us, He will give life to our mortal bodies. Through the power of the Holy Spirit we have life in our bodies. We have healing! By the stripes Jesus bore on His back, we were healed through the power of the Holy Spirit, who gives life to our mortal bodies.

Now let's look at the term Lord Jesus Christ. The word Lord refers to the Father, the supreme authority. Jesus means Savior. Christ refers to the

Anointed One. So, when we talk about our Lord Jesus Christ, we are talking about God, all of God—the supreme authority because the Son cannot do anything without seeing the Father do it, the Son becoming the sacrifice, the Lamb or Savior, being anointed by the Holy Spirit.

Look at John 18:4–9. This passage tells the account of when Judas betrayed Christ. Jesus asked those that had come who they were looking for. They replied, "Jesus of Nazareth."

Then Jesus spoke and said, *"I am He,"* and when He spoke these words, the men who came to get him " *. . . went backward, and fell to the ground"* (Verse 6). Why did this happen? Doesn't this show that just by speaking, the power of Jesus' voice could have killed these men? Jesus could have stopped anyone from doing anything to Him. All He had to do is speak the word and He could have killed them all, but Jesus came to give life. He did this voluntarily. He had the power not to die, but He loved us so much that He was willing to give His life for us.

You may agree with everything you have read thus far, but who is Jesus to you? What about the questions asked in the beginning of this chapter? Let's look together at who Jesus is.

Then Moses said to God, "Indeed, when I come to the children of Israel and say to them, 'the God of your fathers has sent me to you,'
and they say to me, 'What
is His name?,' what shall I say to them?"

And God said to Moses, "I AM
WHO I AM." And He
said, "Thus you shall say to the chil-
dren of Israel, 'I AM
has sent me to you.' "
Exodus 3:13, 14

Let's take a few moments and look at the great I AM.

"I am the God of Abraham, the God of Isaac, the God of Jacob? God is not the God of the dead, but of the living." Matthew 22:32

And Jesus said to them, "I am the bread of life. He who comes to Me shall never hunger, and he who believes in Me shall never thirst."
John 6:35

Then Jesus spoke to them again, saying, "I am the light of the world. He who follows Me shall not walk in darkness, but have the light of life." John 8:12

"I am the Alpha and the Omega, the Beginning and the End," says the Lord, "who is and who was and who is to come, the Almighty."
Revelation 1:8

"I am He who lives, and was dead, and behold, I am alive forevermore. Amen. And I have

the keys of Hades and of Death."
Revelation 1:18

These are just a few references to "I AM. " Do you see the infinite power that Jesus has? What does "I AM" mean to us? It means that He is anything and everything we need in our lives!

who Himself bore our sins in His own body on the tree, that we, having died to sins, might live for righteousness - by whose stripes you were healed. 1Peter 2:24

In righteousness you shall be established; you shall be far from oppression, for you shall not fear; and from terror, for it shall not come near you.
Isaiah 54:14

For His anger is but for a moment, His favor is for life; weeping may endure for a night, but joy comes in the morning."
Psalm 30:5

"Now if God so clothes the grass of the field, which today is, and tomorrow is thrown into the oven, will He not much more clothe you, O you of little faith?"
Matthew 6:30

So they said, "Believe on the Lord Jesus Christ, And you will be saved, you and your household."
Acts 16:31

Is this getting into your spirit? Who is the Lord Jesus Christ? He is the Savior. He is Life. He is Healing. He is the only Way. He is the Truth. He is the Light of the world. He is the Bright and Morning Star, the King of Kings, Lord of Lords, the soon coming King! He is the Lamb of God. He is the ONLY one worthy of all praise and all glory!

The Lord is speaking to you today. He is saying, "Are you lonely? I am your comfort. Are you afraid? I am your shelter. Are you depressed? I am your joy. Are you weary and weak? I am your strength. Are you lost? I am the way. Are you sick? I am your healer. Are you headed for eternity in Hell? I am your salvation. I am the answer to anything and everything you need in your life!"

All you have to do is tell Him what it is you need. You see, God will not force himself on anyone. He knows what you need, but you must come to Him and give Him access to your life. You must be able to let go and let God be what it is you need Him to be. You must talk to Him. He will talk to you. He is not a dead God, but He is alive! Did you hear what I said? God is ALIVE!

Jesus is coming soon to take His bride. He is coming back for His believers. We must be without spot or wrinkle. We must WAKE UP! Many will cry, "Lord, Lord!" but He will not know them. His bride will know Him and He will know His bride. We must be ready for His return!

Jesus said that if we would look to Him, we shall see the Father. We must look to Jesus and follow Him, follow His examples. We must learn to live and follow the leading of the Holy Spirit. In order to live a victorious life, we must have God, all of God, living in us. In Him we live and breathe and have our being. We must surrender to His will. We must let go of our will. We must die to self. He gave all of Himself for us. We need to be willing to give all of us back to Him!

To God be all glory, honor and praise!

Chapter Five:

How to become the Bride of Christ

Why is it so important to understand praise and worship? Why do we need to learn obedience with a thankful heart? Why is today the day for action? What does it mean to become the Bride of Christ?

Jesus is coming soon! It may be before you finish reading this sentence. It may be before you finish reading this book. It may be tonight when you are fast asleep. Jesus can come back for His church, His bride, at any moment! There are things that we must do in order to be ready for this wonderful event! There is going to be a wedding! There are many, many people who think they are going to Heaven. But unless they change their lifestyle, they may find themselves lost for eternity.

Because straight is the gate, and
narrow is the way, which leadeth unto life,
and few there be that find it.
Matthew 7:14(KJV)

The verse prior to this tells of a gate and a broad way, and MANY will choose to follow this path. But this path will lead to destruction! Many will choose the broad way. It is easier to follow. Your flesh will feel better. You may feel that there are fewer battles to fight! Why would the Devil fight you if you aren't doing what God wants you to do? If you aren't following God, the Devil can relax! This is why so many choose the broad road. This is not the choice whether or not to accept Christ into your life. Many who accepted Jesus into their hearts will never see Him!

Are you having trouble swallowing that last statement? Then let me say it again. Many, who have accepted Christ at one time, will never see Him! How can I make that statement?

Because it is written, Be ye holy; for I am holy." 1 Peter 1:16 (KJV)

Where is it written? It was written back in Leviticus 11:44, 45

"For I am the Lord your God. You shall therefore sanctify yourselves and you shall be holy; for I am holy. Neither shall you defile yourselves with any creeping thing that creeps on the earth.
For I am the Lord who brings you up out of the land of Egypt, to be your God. You shall therefore be holy, for I am holy."

. . . Whoever sins has neither seen Him nor known Him. 1 John 3:6

Just as the children of Israel had to sanctify themselves and become holy, so must we. Each one of us must become holy, living a holy lifestyle. We can no longer go through life in a luke-warm state of mind with our "Holy God" Sundays and our "party down" weekends. If we play around in the world, the world will eat us alive! When we accept Jesus into our lives, we have to stop living a sinful life. If we continue in living a sinful life, the Bible clearly says that we never knew Him at all!

I can hear some of you already. "Just a beer once in a while doesn't hurt."

"I just listen to the music, not the words."

Let me ask you this question. Would Jesus be saying these things, listening to this music? The thing we need to realize is that we are to be like Jesus. I don't believe Jesus would walk down the street with his bottle of "Jack" healing those who were afflicted, and teaching of a better life. And I don't think He would walk down the street listening to a lot of music that is being played today. Words that you think you aren't listening to are going into your spirit. And they are speaking death to your soul. I am not saying that all music other than Christian music is bad, but you must look at the message in the song. You must also look at the lifestyle of the artist. Would Jesus approve?

Instead of condoning what they are doing, we

should be praying for them. We should be trying to reach them for Christ. But in order for them to want what we have, we must be different. They need to see that we have something that the world cannot give them. We are to be in this world, but not of it. We need to be the light in the darkness.

Living holy does not mean that you cannot do anything fun. You don't have to be a "home-body," bored to tears. If you like to swim, swim. If you like to play golf, play golf. If you like playing games, sewing, etc., do it! The thing you have to be careful with is this. If it is taking up God's time to do these things, then an adjustment needs to be made. There must be balance. And, when you do these things, make sure that God is getting all the glory and honor He deserves.

Remember, that the way to eternal life is very narrow, and few will go there. Yes, there are things you may have to give up. This is what we call "dying to the flesh," dying to the wants and desires of ourselves. If anything is taking us away from God or the things He wants us to do, we must make adjustments or remove these things. We must not trust our feelings. Our flesh tells us what makes us feel good, but it does not tell us that many of the things that make us feel good are going to kill us in the end!

This is really hard to do sometimes. I know that in my life there were times God told me to do things, and I ignored His voice. There were times that He told me to pray, and I put it off saying, "Lord, I will pray as soon as I am done with this." And I have gone to pray, but I couldn't. Why? Because God had already left! There are things that God would have given me, if I had acted when He told me to act. If I had been obedient, many of the blessings God had for me would have gotten to me sooner! My life may have been very different.

But what if? What if your prayer or my prayer was the prayer that would release healing to a broken body? What if we were someone's last chance to find salvation? What if God wanted to use us to help someone out of fear or depression? WHAT IF?

The bottom line is, you will decide whether or not you will obey God. You decide whether or not you will listen to His voice. However, if you choose not to follow the voice of God, if you don't obey Him, this is sin. Sin must be removed from our lives. Doing the things you like to do is not wrong unless God is telling you to do something else. When what you are doing becomes more important than God, then it becomes wrong.

I protest by your rejoicing which I have in Christ Jesus our Lord, I die daily.
1 Corinthians 15:31 (KJV)

Every day of our lives we have to decide that we will obey the voice of our Lord. Every day we have to decide to obey the Word of God. A phrase I have come to love is this: "It's not a debate, it's a decision!" Every day we must decide to give God glory and honor and praise in everything that happens. EVERY DAY! We must stop debating everything God talks to us about. We must stop fighting the one who wants to give us so much. We must make the decision, every day!

God chose us to be holy. God called our names. He chose us to be His children. In fact, the Bible says that He chose us before He made the world.

According as He hath chosen us in him before the foundations of the world, that we should be holy and without blame before Him in love: Ephesians 1:4 (KJV)
Husbands, love your wives, just as Christ also loved the church and gave Himself for it, that He might sanctify and cleanse it with the washing of water by the word, that He might present it to Himself a glorious church, not having spot or wrinkle or any such thing, but that it should be holy and without blemish. Ephesians 5:25–27

Let's examine for a moment the parable of the ten virgins found in Matthew 25:1–13. There were ten girls, virgins, who were friends with a girl who was about to get married. The Bible says that five of the girls were foolish and five of them were wise. The five girls that were wise carried their lamps and extra oil, in case they needed it. The five that were foolish took their lamps, but they did not carry extra oil.

It was customary at this time for the girls to

go to the bride's home and wait for the bridegroom to come and take them to the wedding. They would go and light their lamps so the groom would know where to pick them up. Well, it was getting late and the girls got tired, so they went to sleep.

Around midnight there came a yell that the groom was leaving his house. He was coming for his bride. This of course woke up all the girls. Upon awakening, the girls noticed that the flames were getting weak in their lamps. The five who did not have extra oil asked the five with oil if they could loan them some, but they were refused. If the five wise girls shared the oil, there may not have been enough for any of them to last until the groom arrived. The five foolish girls were told to hurry and go buy some oil.

While they were gone buying oil, the bridegroom reached the bride's home. The five wise girls went out to meet him. Then they all left for the wedding. The five girls who had gone to buy oil missed their ride and arrived at the wedding late. But, when they got there, they were not allowed to enter the ceremony because the groom did not know them. These girls were friends of the bride; the groom did not know them.

After Jesus told this parable, he said,

> *Watch therefore, for ye know neither the day nor the hour wherein the Son of man cometh. Matthew 25:13 (KJV)*

Let's apply this to our lives. Many Christians were filled up at one time. Their "fire" for God was burning strong. They wanted to win the world for Christ. But over time, the things they had learned and felt became old, stagnant. They were no longer walking in the will of the Father. All their zest for God and their hunger for God had been used up. They no longer read the Bible. They no longer prayed. They no longer sought God in all things the way they did in the beginning.

How does this happen? It is human nature! Think about it. What do people do when they get something new? They use it all the time. They feel happy that they have it, but after a little time, the newness wears off. It doesn't get used as much. Then they start looking for something else, something better and something bigger. The same thing happens to Christians.

When you accept Jesus into your life, you are filled with joy and hope. You want to know everything about Him. You read your Bible, pray, and go to church, but little by little you stop reading as much. You stop praying as much. Maybe, you even stop going to church as much. You begin relying on the pastor to get fed. You begin to rely on the pastor to be the soul winner.

We need to be fed more than once or twice a week. We need to be fed daily. What I have found is that there is always something new, something bigger, something better in the Word of God. There can always be excitement, every day! How can we be fed daily and grow daily if we don't come to the Bread of Life, daily?

Another reason for us to seek Him daily is this: Many pastors will not preach on the things that make us grow. There are a lot of feelings to deal with when God is changing a person, and the preacher doesn't want to offend anyone. They are afraid that people will leave their church along with their money. So the church receives "old manna," things you once needed but have outgrown. You cannot always rely on someone else to feed your soul. Growing means pain! Maybe that's why they're called "growing pains"! It hurts to grow up. God shows us things we don't want to deal with. Stop crying about the preacher stepping on your toes! Instead, thank God. He is showing you what needs to be fixed in your life in order to have a closer walk with Him!

The flame has gone out for millions. The flame is weak in millions more. They need more oil. They need more fuel for their flame. They need to have a reserve of oil. This is one reason why people fall away from God. The oil is the power, the fuel of the Holy Spirit. We must spend time in the Word and in prayer. We must spend time with the Holy Spirit. We must put the Word in our hearts, our holding tanks.

If we spend time in the Word, if we spend time in prayer, if we spend time getting to know the Almighty, when trials come, we can stand strong. When temptation is before us, we can overcome it. We will have a reserve of praise for those times we don't feel like praising Him. We will have a reserve of strength to push through to the end, even though we are tired. We won't be weak in the knees, but rather, we will be able to withstand the storms of life, unwavering in our faith. We can stand strong like the tree that is planted by the water, and we shall not be moved!

God is strength. God is joy. God is love. God is protection. God is the great I AM. We must learn to live and breathe God. We must draw close to Him. We must love and obey Him. This is how we become the Bride of Christ, when every word He speaks is life to us. Whenever He asks us to do something, we should be eager to do it. All we want to do is please Him. He must be the reason we live. He must be the most important person in our lives. And everything we say and do should bring glory and honor to His name.

Don't let your lamp run out of oil. Don't let the flame go out. Stop eating old stale food. Eat from the table He has prepared for you. Drink from the life-giving water. Be ready when He comes to take us home to be with Him. Don't miss your way to the wedding. Jesus can come at any moment. How sure are you that you will be there?

Jesus is the only answer to all the problems in life. Jesus is the only way to happiness and freedom. He is looking for you. Let your light shine bright!

Chapter Six:

The Covenant

There are two sides to every story. Now comes the time when you will decide which gate you will enter. You will decide which path to follow. You can walk to please your flesh, or you can walk to please your spirit. You can choose to listen and obey the voice of God, or you can choose to listen to those along the way, those who wish to divert your attention off the straight and narrow into separation from God Almighty for all eternity. Some of you will have a debate with yourself. But remember, it's not a debate, it's a decision.

They will use phrases like, "Just one more time," or, "It's just a little fun. It's so sweet, just taste." But Jesus said, "Watch therefore, for ye know neither the day nor the hour the Son of man cometh." (Matthew 25:13)

Jesus gave us the way to be able to talk directly to God. I am so thankful that we can go before God ourselves. Still, many of us stay out in the courtyard and offer our praise. We still wait for the priest or the pastor to do most of the work. I understand that we must come to God to ask for forgiveness. No one else can do this for us, but what about reading the scriptures, learning about what God wants for our lives? What about prayer? What about seeking the answers for our daily lives by seeking Him? Why is it that we put so much faith and trust in evangelists, preachers and teachers? Why do we think that they are the only ones God speaks to? Do we need them? Yes! Do they help us? Yes! They have been given this position to teach us and help us grow in our understanding, but it is our job to get to know God and what His will is for our lives.

There must be a balance in our lives. There must be a balance between being taught and studying the Word, just as there should be a balance in praise and prayer. There has to be a balance between living our daily life in this world and preparing for our life in Heaven.

God desires for each of us to freely give ourselves to Him. He desires that we do all things with a heart of thankfulness. God demands obedience. God demands all of the praise and glory. God is all power and all life. Without Him we are dead! Why not freely bow on your knees and worship His Majesty - the Lord Jesus Christ. For, you see, the day is coming when every knee will bow and every tongue will confess that Jesus is Lord! God wants us to do this voluntarily, but if you don't choose to confess this, there is a day coming when, whether you want to or not, you will bow down and you will confess Jesus is Lord.

God is a covenant God. Are you willing to enter a covenant with Him? This is not a commitment. A commitment is something you plan to do, but it is often forgotten or broken. A covenant, on the other hand, is a contract. When you make a covenant with God, you are bound by the terms of the agreement you make with God. God has written a contract from Genesis 1:1 through Revelation 22:21. All of the answers for life are in the contract. In it are all the promises, stipulations, terms and conditions. God is bound by the guidelines that He has set. He has made promises to us and He cannot go back on His word.

Why don't we see these promises being fulfilled? It is because we aren't doing what the contract calls for us to do. We are not following the terms or conditions. In order to receive the promise, we must obey the laws or principles for that promise. We have not made that covenant with God. As I said before, we want God to live up to His promises unconditionally. Yet we don't want to have to do anything to get it. There is always something God asks us to do in obedience in order to reach the promise.

Then Jesus said to His followers, "If people want to follow me, they must give up what they want. They must be willing even to give up their lives to follow me. Those who want to save their lives will give up true life, and those who give up their lives for me will have

true life. It is worth nothing for them to have the whole world if they lose their souls. They could never pay enough to buy back their souls. The Son of Man will come again with his Father's glory and with his angels. At that time, he will reward them for what they have done."
Matthew 16:24–27 (NCV)

Now is the time to get rid of anger, rage, malicious behavior, slander and dirty language. Don't lie to each other, for you have stripped off your old evil nature and all its wicked deeds. In its place you have clothed yourself with a brand-new nature that is continually being renewed as you learn more and more about Christ, who created this new nature with-in you.
Colossians 3:8–10 (NLT)

Children, obey your parents in the Lord, for this is right. "Honor your father and mother," which is the first commandment with promise: "That it may be well with you and you may live long on the earth."
Ephesians 6:1–3

Therefore, having these promises, beloved, let us cleanse ourselves from all filthiness of the flesh and spirit, perfecting holiness in the fear of God. 2 Corinthians 7:1

Do you want to have a power-filled life? Do you want a blessed life? Do you want to have a happy life? If so, then you must learn to live by the principles God has laid out in His Word, to worship and praise, to obey with a thankful heart. That is all that the creator of the universe is asking for. Is that too much to ask? After all, if God had not created man, we wouldn't even be here. Without the creator, there is no creation.

Even Jesus had to obey the will of the Father. Otherwise, there would not be salvation for us. When Jesus said, **" . . . Not as I will, but as You will"** (Matthew 26:39), he was being obedient to the Father. Throughout His life Jesus said that he could not do anything without seeing the Father do it.

Jesus not only died for us, but He rose from the dead, and the power of the Holy Spirit which raised Jesus from the dead is here for us today! Jesus ascended into Heaven to sit at the right hand of the Father to intercede on our behalf. When He left this earth, He left the Holy Spirit here to teach us and guide us. All so we could have a chance to spend eternity with our creator, our God. He is the only one true God. The only living God! And all He asks us to do is to obey Him and give Him praise in all situations in our lives, continually.

Stop bringing God down to your level. Stop putting limitations on the power of our God. It is time to move up to God's level. It is time to let God be God. At this moment God knows exactly what it is you need, but, you must reach out to Him. You must give Him permission; give Him access to your life.

You must call out to Him. Call on His name and then let Him do His work in your life.

Will you enter into a covenant relationship with the Lord? He is just waiting for you to give yourself to Him. He wants to bless you in bigger and better ways than you could ever imagine. The human mind cannot fathom the depth of God's love for us. We can not even begin to imagine what God has in store for those who will worship and praise His holy name.

Remember, it is not a debate, it is a decision. Decide now to enter a covenant relationship with the Almighty God. Decide now to obey Him with a thankful heart. Choose today whom you will serve, *" . . . But as for me and my house, we will serve the Lord."* (Joshua 24:15)

GLORY TO THE LAMB!
WORTHY IS THE LAMB THAT WAS SLAIN!
GLORY TO GOD IN THE HIGHEST!
HIS MERCY ENDURES FOREVER! Amen!

Gregg Spilker
537 Parsons Road
Christiana, TN 37037–6129
Or e-mail:singermanone@aol.com
Please include your prayer requests and comments when you write.

or order more copies of this book at

TATE PUBLISHING, LLC

127 East Trade Center Terrace
Mustang, Oklahoma 73064

(888) 361 - 9473

Tate Publishing, LLC

www.tatepublishing.com